# To Make the Moment Last

# To Make the Moment Last

## The Story of the Incredible Jades

William E. Thrasher Jr.

To Make the Moment Last
The Story of the Incredible Jades

iUniverse books may be ordered through booksellers or by contacting:

iUniverse
1663 Liberty Drive
Bloomington, IN 47403
www.iuniverse.com
1-800-Authors (1-800-288-4677)

Because of the dynamic nature of the Internet, any web addresses or
links contained in this book may have changed since publication and
may no longer be valid. The views expressed in this work are solely those
of the author and do not necessarily reflect the views of the publisher,
and the publisher hereby disclaims any responsibility for them.

Any people depicted in stock imagery provided by Thinkstock are
models, and such images are being used for illustrative purposes only.
Certain stock imagery © Thinkstock.

ISBN: 978-1-4917-7466-3 (sc)
ISBN: 978-1-4917-7467-0 (e)

Library of Congress Control Number: 2015915065

Print information available on the last page.

iUniverse rev. date: 10/29/2015

To David, Granvel, and Leonard, whose
moments have transcended to eternity, and
to Scooter, John, Yacky, Joe, Cheryl, Dennis,
Patrick, and Ruben, without whom there
would not have been a moment at all.

# Contents

# Foreword

William, I personally thank you for going back to the magic that started me on this journey of notes, beats, and measures, and of the ups and downs of the business of music. To those of you who dare to dream the dream of music: if you believe it, you can see it, and if you see it, you can achieve it. It seems hard, but it is the sacrifice given of oneself to become a musician or singer. One of the most touching scriptures that has helped me through the years is Hebrews 11:1: "Now, faith is the substance of things hoped for, evidence of things not seen." This business will lead you to pray. But enjoy the excitement of the classmates and friends whose stories are told here. Read about how we dared to try.

In closing, I'll offer one more scripture, Luke 10:7: "A laborer is worthy of his hire." That's the lesson we learned on our first gig. So here is how the journey started. Enjoy!

George "Scooter" Mitchell

Special thanks to Scooter, Yacky, and Joe, whose memories helped me bring the moments forward, and to my family and friends, who encouraged me throughout the process.

# CHAPTER 1

# The Birth of a Moment

I can't really say that what we had was a dream, at least not in the true sense of the word. No, what we had was a moment. It was a moment that lasted for only a couple of summers, but that couple of summers seemed like a lifetime.

It was the winter of '67. We were at school, just playing around in the band room, and John Reeves started playing on the piano. John was truly a talented guy. He could play almost any kind of instrument; he had talent coming out of his ears. He started playing this boogie-woogie riff, and David Bynum—we called him "Brubeck" because he was so cool and played such a smooth horn—jumped in on his trumpet.

There are artists, and then there are mechanics. David was an artist. You could hear the blending of light and color in every note he played. Granvel Hadley followed David as the second trumpet. Granvel was more of an artistic mechanic. While he was not as smooth as David, his playing was very precise, with a crisp, solid sound.

Scooter (George Mitchell) picked up the beat with the snare drum. Scooter had just the drive and energy that we needed. He was laid-back, but he was also serious about the music. You could feel the rhythm flowing through his sticks, and it made the music infectious. Yacky (Donald Jenkins) and Dennis Grant added a mean trombone section. They were both very good trombonists, and there was always a little competition between them. Yacky, however, was more committed to the sound, and sometimes he could be very intense when it came to getting the music right.

I brought up the rear as the woodwind section, with my clarinet. I felt like a lost ball in high grass, but at least I was there. I was more like the true mechanic, a real nuts-and-bolts kind of musician. I might not have been as creative as the other guys, but once I got it together—the music, that is—I was hard to beat.

It wasn't just the sound that made that moment special—although the sound was getting funky. There was also this *feeling*. It was the sense that something special was beginning that gave birth to what we would later call the Incredible Jades.

We were having fun—and man, were we getting down. Everybody tried to show off by playing his own little solo. I don't know if "St. James Infirmary" was ever the same again.

When my turn came, I didn't hit that groove like the other guys. It just wasn't funky enough to say yes. But there we were, making a sound. And even with my lack of funkiness, it was a sound that we liked. So every morning, we would get to the band room early, before first hour, and work on that sound. I tried to make my clarinet work, because I had always thought that the instrument had a cool, smooth sound. I remember the first time I heard the clarinet played by a professional. It was at the Main Theater in downtown Little Rock, Arkansas. During intermission, a clip of Pete Fountain came on the screen; he was walking through a garden at night, playing "A Stranger on the Shore." I thought that was so cool. It was, and that was what I wanted to sound like. But now, with the loud trumpets, even louder trombones, and of course Scooter's beating of the drum, it was just too overpowering for my funky-less clarinet. So after a week of not finding my groove, I went home and told my parents I had to have a saxophone. And not just any saxophone, but a tenor sax, because it was a big enough "axe" (that's what all the professionals called their instruments) to keep up with the rest of the guys. And I told them that if they would sign for it, I would pay for it. And so they did.

As you can imagine, the first time I played my "axe," I was not prepared for the squawks and squeaks that came out the other end. Nor was I prepared for the abuse to my bottom lip—wow, was it sore! But convinced that that was the sound that I wanted, I worked at it until I got it right. No, not *right*—until I got it funky! After all, Pete Fountain wasn't playing Motown or James Brown. But Junior Walker was, and so was Maceo Parker, James Brown's lead sax man.

One of the guys had heard about a lead guitar player, Joe Thomas, who was supposed to be hot, and when we finally got to hear Joe, he wasn't just hot—he was smoking. If David was an artist, Joe was a gourmet chef: the way he made those strings sound was simply sizzling!

Our sound was getting better and better, but there was still something missing: there wasn't a bottom to the sound. What we needed was a bass guitar. So Yacky decided that he would teach himself to play. He tackled that bass with an intense passion. You could look at his face and see every note he was playing, and when he hit a bad note, the expression on his face made you glad there were no mirrors around. But true to his dedication, it wasn't long before he was laying down bass lines with the best of them.

Now we were playing music. The sound was whole. It was vibrant. It was strong. And yet it was funky, and thanks to Yacky, it now had bottom— gut-bucket bottom (that's what professionals called a real funky sound). We picked up a couple of male vocalists—Patrick Eubanks, a Sam & Dave-style singer, and Ruben Johnson, who had more of a Lou Rawls kind of groove—and to round things out, we got a female vocalist, Cheryl Moore, who not only was good- looking but also had Aretha Franklin in her pocket.

There is a nationally syndicated radio personality who describes his radio prowess as "talent on loan from God." I think that is an apt description of the talents that made up the Incredible Jades.

With our parts in place, we were now ready to get serious. The caterpillar (the moment) had finally shed its cocoon.

# CHAPTER 2

# All This Music and No Place to Play

We had music coming out of our ears. Motown certainly was living up to its image as Hitsville, USA. Every week there was a new chart topper (that's what professionals called a new top-ten hit song). They were manufacturing songs as quickly as GM was manufacturing cars. The hits were coming so fast it was hard to choose which new one to learn first. And if that wasn't challenging enough, finding a place big enough to rehearse in was even tougher. But it wasn't for lack of trying.

We first tried rehearsing in my family's basement. My brothers and sisters loved it, especially my baby brother, Greg, who at three years old zoned in on Scooter. When Greg saw Scooter play those drums, he was like a deer in the headlights. I wish I could say that our neighbors were as receptive. They were ... well, let's just say that after a couple of late-night sessions, it became a them-or-us kind of thing and so we got booted out.

The next place we tried was Yacky's. His house was up on a hill, and at the back of his property, there was a steep drop-off that acted like a valley. As you can imagine, the valley amplified the sound, and in no time at all, we were again looking for another place to play.

We tried it at Joe's house, and while we got no complaints, we didn't have quite enough space to fit all our equipment and practice our dance steps too.

My dad, who was then the director of the South End Boys' Club, saw that we really needed room, so he allowed us to practice there. Then we were, as they say, off to the races.

By February we had learned quite a few songs and needed a way to test our sound on the public. So for my sister Pearl's eighteenth and my seventeenth birthday—February 20 and 28, respectively—my parents allowed us to celebrate with a party at the Boys' Club. We invited all our friends from school and the neighborhood, but we didn't tell them that our group would provide the music.

I'll never forget that Friday night. It was cold, cold, cold outside. Did I mention that it was cold? The kids started trickling in slowly at first, and we were afraid that not many were really going to come. You must understand that it was *cold* outside. Plus, who in their right minds would show up on time for a party just so it would start on time? The rule for party going was the more fashionably late you were, the better.

Finally a crowd began to develop. We took the stage to what we thought was going to be a rough audience, because they were ready for the top ten to spin on the hi-fi, and what they saw was a bunch of amateurs they knew but had never heard. Were we nervous? Are you kidding? We were scared out of our minds. But we had practiced; we were ready. And even though we heard some of them making jokes, we tuned up our axes, and the next sound they heard was "Papa's Got a Brand New Bag." Well, as cold as it was on the outside, the joint was just as hot on the inside. Kids were ringing wet, breaking out in a cold sweat from so much boogalooing, camel walking, and cool jerking. Every time we broke out with a new top-ten, the girls would scream and the guys would holler. We weren't just good—we were *goooood*!

The party was a smash. The kids loved us, and for the next few weeks we were the talk of the school and the neighborhood. The butterfly (the moment) was surely beginning to emerge.

# CHAPTER 3

# Our Day Will Come

With our debut successfully behind us, we were confident that we could stand on stage and deliver. Now we had only two problems: figuring out what were we going to call ourselves and deciding what our theme song would be. You must understand the times we were living in. It was the late sixties. The black music world had been emancipated. There were two major record labels that dominated R&B music:

Motown and Stax Records. Motown had artists such as the Miracles, the Temptations, the Supremes, Stevie Wonder, Marvin Gaye and Tammi Terrell, the Four Tops, Gladys Night & the Pips, and Junior Walker & the All Stars. Stax had such legends as Booker T. & the MG's, Sam & Dave, Isaac Hayes, and of course Otis Redding. And there were the king and queen of soul, James Brown and Aretha Franklin. These were just a few of the giants who were topping the charts week after week back then, and if you called yourself a band and you wanted to survive, you had better be ready to play their music and imitate their sound.

As young and naive as we were, we really understood the times we were in, and we knew that if you were in the entertainment business, you needed a name that separated you from your competition. It also had to have a good ring to it; it had to be cool and project coolness. Somehow, you had to convey that your band—on any given night, on any stage— could bring it. You had to have a theme song that let the people know that it was you on the stage and that the familiar theme was your signature presence on the stage.

David provided the theme song. From the very first day we started, David knew, maybe before anybody else did, that we could be something special. All we needed was a chance and some hard work. That's what he believed, and he made believers out of the rest of us. He said that if we worked hard enough and truly believed, our day would come. That's a lot of wisdom from someone so young, but he was right—and there the theme was, right in front of us: "Our Day Will Come."

As for our name, we knew that in our own minds, our sound was "incredible," but what to put with it? We wanted to rock the crowds, but the Incredible Rocks? Nah! The Incredible Sounds? Nope! The Incredibles? Get real. How about the Incredible Jades? Yeah! That worked. Not only was jade a rock, but it was a precious stone of great value. The ancients believed that it possessed positive power, and we knew one day we would too. Hey, the name stuck—and the rest is history.

So we were finally a full-fledged group, with a name and theme song to boot. We had a growing repertoire and enough energy to put the Energizer Bunny out of business. Watch out, world—the butterfly (the moment) was about to take flight.

# CHAPTER 4

# We Found a Hole in the Wall

We needed a gig. (That's what professionals called a paid performance or engagement.) We were becoming somewhat popular, but we wanted to do more than just give out freebies. We wanted to get paid. We *needed* to get paid. We were in hock for a lot of equipment: amps, drum set, bass guitar, microphones and speakers, and don't forget my sax too. We needed a gig.

What we found was a hole in the wall. (That's what professionals called a juke joint or nightclub that wasn't much bigger than a hole in the wall.) It was called the Owl's Club. Looking back on it now, I see that it really lived up to its name: anything bigger than an owl could just about forget it. But hey, it was our first gig, our first professional job. We were going to get paid! As far as we were concerned, it was a grand ballroom.

We were engaged to play that Friday night from 9:00 p.m. to 1:00 a.m. So we loaded up all our equipment and went over early to set up and get ready for our gig. The stage was barely big enough to fit everything on it—boy, was it close—but we made it fit, deciding that we would have to forget about our dance routines and just settle for playing the music.

At 9:00 p.m. sharp, the spotlight (all they had was one) came on. The announcer said, "Ladies and gentlemen, for your listening entertainment, for the first time on this or any other stage, we are proud to present the Incredible Jades!" Our day had come! We hit the theme song and never looked back.

By midnight we had played everything we knew at least twice and were going around for the third time. Of course by then, all the Owl's Club patrons were feeling no pain, and I don't think they really noticed or cared. They were feeling good and having a big ol' time—that is, until a shot rang out. It was one of those too-much-liquor-and-not-enough-sense  moments. Fortunately for us, it was short-lived, but it was scary nonetheless. The entire band cleared the stage, or so we thought, trying to find the safest spot behind the stage to crawl into.

You know how when you go into a dark room and cut the lights on, the roaches scatter? Well, that was us. Funny thing, though: while we were ducking and dodging, we could hear the bass guitar just a-blowing and going. When the shot rang out, Yacky had had his back to the audience and was just really into the sound of his bass. He was in another world, all by himself—just him and his bass. We kept screaming, "Yacky! Yacky!" He finally turned and saw that he was on the stage all by himself, and then he saw us in the wings, beckoning for him to get off the stage.

Well, by then it was all over. The shooting had stopped, and everyone was leaving the club. The guy who had rented out the club for the night and booked us for the gig came over and told us the good news and the bad news. The good news was that nobody got hurt. The bad news was that since he had to refund everyone's money, we weren't going to get paid. That was when we learned the fine art of the gentleman's agreement. (That's what professionals called a verbal contract with nothing in writing.) With nothing in writing, we didn't have a leg to stand on. We called my dad (I called him Daddy William) and Granvel's dad (Big Jim Hadley), and they talked with the owner of the club, who said that the guy who booked us would meet them the next day on Ninth Street. Daddy William said not to expect much, and he was right. But the good news was we had learned a very valuable lesson: always get your contracts in writing, and make sure that the responsible party's signature is on the bottom line.

The next day, the owner of the club called my dad and told him that he was so impressed with our group that he wanted to book us directly. So the next weekend, we were back at the hole in the wall again, but this time we had our contract in hand and we did get paid.

That was the second of many weekends to come that we performed at the Owl's Club. We became one the club's most consistently requested groups, and our reputation was spreading like wildfire. The butterfly (moment) had morphed into a rocket and was heading for the moon.

# CHAPTER 5

# The Shortest Distance between Two Points: The Jade Mobile

While it may be true that the shortest distance between two points is a straight line, getting from point A to point B proved to be quite challenging.

The thing about becoming a group—and not just any group, but one that would be in constant demand—was making sure that we all showed up at the same time, safe and sound. While we were all driving age, we did not own one car among us. We got friends and family to get us to the gigs that were close and local, but we never knew who would get there first or in time to set things up. The logistics were a growing nightmare. We needed a solution, and we needed one fast.

Joe's dad came up with the mother of all solutions: a 1940s Cadillac stretch limousine. It was long, sleek, black, and shiny, with chrome side running boards and moonglow rims. It could seat nine passengers comfortably, and you could squeeze in two more if necessary. It had dark-tinted windows that added to its mystique. The limo also had a hitch on the back so that we could haul a trailer for our instruments and equipment.

One moment we were getting around catch as catch can, and the next we were riding in style. When we pulled up at a gig, everyone would stop and take notice. You could hear folks say, "The Jades are here!" How cool was that? It was so cool that we had to give the limo a name. *Batman* was a popular TV show back then, and he had his Batmobile. Well, we would not be outdone; we christened our monster ride the Jade Mobile. It was, in a word, real *cooooool*. What a chick magnet—girls would line up for days for a chance to ride in the Jade Mobile!

I had always heard the old saying "too hot to trot." Well, now I knew just what that meant. We were so hot, we were melting!

# CHAPTER 6

# Overnight Success

As rare as it may be, there really is such a thing as an overnight success. By the time summer rolled around, we couldn't keep up with all our bookings. If one of us got a call to perform, we would say yes without checking to see what commitments we already had. The end result of that was too much overbooking, which was really getting out of hand.

The demands of our "overnight success" made it abundantly clear that we were not equipped to handle the business side of what we were becoming. If success was teaching us anything, it was that to whom much is given, much is required.

So Joe's dad took on that responsibility. It was a no-brainer to us, because he was already serving as our chaperone and that was the logical next step. I'm not sure if Mr. Thomas really knew what he was getting himself into, and I'm not sure if he was smart to do it or just crazy, but he made it work. As I look back on those days, I find it unbelievable how well he managed two handfuls of teenaged boys and a young lady, provided our transportation, kept our schedule, and managed our bookings. He was quite a guy.

We were in high demand, on stage and off. Girls were coming out of the woodwork, and even a nerd like me had to fight to keep them off. (Of course, I didn't fight very hard.) As our popularity continued to grow, so did our following. It got to be so tough that at some engagements, we would have to arrive earlier than usual just to avoid the deluge of fans. (Well, that's the way I remember it). We even had to be careful about whom we smiled at when we were on stage. You see, from a fan's point of view, a smile was the equivalent of a commitment. Sometimes we could hear the girls saying, "He smiled at me first!" "No, he smiled at *me* first!" and when we would take a break, we sometimes were confronted by rival fans demanding to know at whom we were smiling and, if we'd smiled at the wrong one, just what we'd meant.

Yes, the burdens of being an overnight success were hard. It was a tough job, but the Jades were incredibly able to do it!

# CHAPTER 7
# Not a Perfect World

A few things happened that really put our moment to the test. First Dennis, our trombone player, decided to pursue other interests and left the group. Then Patrick Eubanks got a chance to tour with Up with People, and Ruben Johnson's parents felt that even with a chaperone, Ruben was too young to keep the hours our gigs demanded, so they made him quit. Later that fall, John Reed would follow Patrick on tour with Up with People.

What were we going to do? Who could we get to replace our male vocalists and eventually our keyboard player as well? We'd thought we could do nothing wrong. We'd felt like we had the world by a string, when in fact we were floating in a bubble and the fickle finger of fate was poking a hole in it. In a perfect world, we would not have problems like this. We quickly learned that ours was not a perfect world. Not only was our world not perfect; it was beginning to unravel. We needed help—a whole bunch of help.

What we got was nothing short of a miracle: Leonard Givens. Leonard could play the keyboards. In fact, he could make the keyboards sing. Watching him play was like watching Chuck Berry and Little Richard rolled into one. And did he have a voice! He had an unbelievable range; he could handle any artist, from Otis Redding to Smokey Robinson. Leonard was indeed the complete package. With the addition of Leonard to the group, our popularity and success just continued to grow. It might not have been a perfect world, but it was still our world to command!

# Chapter 8

# Hot Fun in the Summertime

As the summer rolled on, we really got to test our mettle: we competed in the Battle of the Bands, which pitted the most popular rock-and-roll groups against the most popular rhythm-and-blues bands. The competitions were wild and crazy and just a blast.

One of them took place on the Fourth of July at the War Memorial Stadium. By then I was driving, and

I wanted to take my girlfriend, Vera Hodge, so I asked my grandparents, Willie and Minerva Jones, if I could take their car. Would you believe they wanted to come along? I actually doubled-dated with my grandparents! Imagine this: Vera and I were in the backseat of my grandparents' '59 Cadillac, and they were in the front, acting like they were really our contemporaries, out on a date too. I saw a side of my grandparents that I had never seen before—especially my grandmother. I had no idea she knew how to have fun. Well, they had a ball.

I don't know if it was just me or if it was the setting, which was so cool in the midst of the heat; all I knew was we were having hot fun in the summertime. Of course, the Incredible Jades had its following, and when it came time for the audience to let the judges know whom they liked, our fans were large and in charge. The screaming was so loud it could be heard five blocks away. There were two groups that got the most audience response: the Incredible Jades and the Merging Traffic, the most popular white group in the area. The judges said it was too close to call, but if Vera and my grandparents were hoarse from all their cheering, as far as I was concerned, we had won.

There was no question that we had great chemistry. It was the right formula, the perfect combination of sight, sound, and movement. We worked very hard at making everything fit just right, and sometimes we got it dead-on. One such time was a performance for a regional black teen beauty pageant held at the Downtowner Motor Inn. There were young ladies from as far north as Oklahoma and as far south as Texas. We had been hired to be the stage band, providing backup for those young ladies who performed singing and/or dancing routines, as well as providing musical entertainment after the competition was over. I think what impressed the crowd, in addition to our music, was how well we were choreographed. We had a different move for every song.

The highlight of the evening came when we played "Summertime." At the end of a riveting solo to end the song, David hit a high note, and the rest of us fell to our knees at precisely the same time—and the place exploded. The girls raced up on stage and started tearing away at our clothes as though we were true rock stars. We barely got out of there with our pants on. Were we hot, or what!

One of the best gauges of our success was being invited to play Sunday afternoon concerts at the Dunbar Community Center with all the local notables. There were the Art Porter Trio, Henry Shed, T-Roy Betton and the Playboys, the Ralph Porter Trio, Thomas East, and, last but not least, the Incredible Jades. We had youth, we had energy, we had moves, and we had the sound. Forget the moon; our moment was headed for the stars!

# CHAPTER 9

# For the Sake of Posterity

With the success that we were having, it wasn't long before we were legends in our own minds. Our heads had gotten bigger than breadbaskets. We started having visions of stardom, and we knew that to make that happen, we needed to make a record.

Whenever a new hit song came out, we would go to Soul Brothers Record Shop to get it and add it to our ever-growing repertoire. Mr. Lee Anthony was the owner of Soul Brothers, and he not only sold records but also had begun making them too. At first he did not have a studio, but he did have some pretty good equipment. So we arranged for him to come to the Boys' Club after his shop closed and make a recording of us.

While Mr. Anthony was setting up, Daddy William happened to be there, observing how Mr. Anthony was arranging his microphones. He asked Mr. Anthony if he could suggest the best way to arrange microphones, and for the rest of the night, the two of them collaborated on how to get the most out of the equipment. Years later, Mr. Anthony would tell me how much he learned about recording from working with my dad that one night.

Well, the first recording was great, as far as we were concerned. Even though we only recorded tunes that were already hits, it was still exciting to sit and hear what we really sounded like. After we finished feeding our egos, Mr. Anthony pointed out the tons of mistakes we were making blending our sounds together. He said we sounded like we were afraid we weren't going to be heard, when all we really had to do was make sure our mics were positioned properly, and of course we needed to play with more volume control. We took his advice and tried to put it into practice the next time we recorded with him. Later, when he built his own recording studio, the advice that he had given us made a lot more sense and improved the quality of our sound tremendously.

Throughout the remainder of the summer, between our gigs and our regular work, we had several recording sessions. Each one was a true learning experience. We even tried writing some original material, which we also recorded. One tune that we wrote was called "Water." The lyrics were as crazy as the title. It wasn't top-ten material, but at least it showed that we could be original. I think we decided to leave the music writing to Motown and James Brown for the time being. One thing was for sure, though: with all the recordings we made, we felt sure that we had captured our moment for posterity.

## CHAPTER 10

# There's No Business Like Show Business

By the fall of '67, we had become a well-oiled machine, having played in just about every popular venue in the region. We were hot and we knew it.

When we got back to school, we were big-time seniors—big-time seniors ready to strut our stuff. The principal, Mr. Edwin Hawkins, called us into his office and told us that there would be no stuff strutting at his school. He said he knew that we were fairly popular, but we should not let our popularity go to our heads. That was good advice, but it was about three months too late. He also said that the word was we were pretty good. Of course, that just made our heads swell even more. He told us that he wanted us to perform for the first all-boys' assembly of the year, and if that went well, he might have something else for us to do.

We must have done pretty well, because we played not just for the assembly but for the homecoming dance too.

The head of the speech and drama department, Mrs. Vivian Hegwood, recruited us for her senior-class presentation of *Showboat*, which put on several performances at our school and then went on tour to other schools, as well.

Something new in the fall was the addition of uniforms to our stage personae. Talk about flashy— we made the sun think about not shining. We found shimmering metallic-green tops that looked like Christmas trees with icicles on them. I can imagine what you are thinking, but remember, that's what show business is all about. And we showed out.

Then the principal did something that shocked even us: he told us that he was going to call a surprise all-school assembly, and he wanted us to entertain the entire school. This was to be the Mount Everest performance of our brief lives. When Mr. Hawkins announced the assembly, he said that he would not state the purpose but expected everyone to be there.

When the day finally came, we were so excited we could hardly contain ourselves. We wore coats and jackets over our uniforms so no one could tell what was going on, and when the students began to assemble, we joined them in the audience. Suddenly the lights went off in the auditorium, and you could hear a pin drop. Then out of the dark silence came Scooter's drumbeat. Yacky jumped up out of his seat, ran on to the stage, picked up his bass, and joined Scooter's funky beat. Joe came next and added his signature rhythm. Every time one of us got up, the crowd would go wild. Leonard was next, followed by David, then Granvel, and finally me. By this time, I think the principal was having second thoughts about the surprise assembly, because even the teachers were having a good time.

When we were all on stage, we took our jackets and coats off to reveal our new, shiny costumes. The girls were screaming and falling out everywhere.

For one hour we played a Motown, James Brown, and Aretha Franklin revue. I believe the stars themselves would have been proud of us. Then it dawned on me that I would never again see a time when our moment shined so bright. There was no business like show business.

# CHAPTER 11

# The Tapestry of the Nightlife

It is amazing to me that the older you get, the more different things seem than the way they first appeared to you. Let me give you an example. When I was just a small child, there was a hill in front of my house that the neighborhood kids could roll down for days. We had so much fun rolling down that hill. No one could tell us that it rose only two feet off the ground. To my brothers and sisters and me, it was a mountain. Since that time, I have seen anthills that would put our "hill" to shame.

So it was with the nightlife around our town back in the late sixties. Nowadays, it would not be much of a stretch to say that if you have been to one club, you've been to them all. Back then, that was not the case. Each club had its own uniqueness about it. The atmosphere at the Owl's Club in North Little Rock you would not find at the Diplomat down on Ninth Street in Little Rock. And what you found at the Diplomat you would not find at the Beverly Gardens down in Sweet Home, Arkansas. Each club had a different flavor.

The Owl's Club catered to a very earthy crowd of people. There was one couple we saw every Friday night we performed there. They were always among the first people there and the last to leave, and they would come dressed to the nines, walking hand in hand. It was obvious that they were very much in love. He would be all smiles, like a proud peacock. She would be tucked up under his arm, as though he were her great protector. By closing time, they would have torn each other's clothes to shreds, and he would be dragging her out feetfirst. It was exactly like that every weekend, and no one could tell them that they did not have a good time. They were working class and proud of it.

At the Diplomat, you would not find couples like that. Instead you would find the hip dudes and their fine ladies—folks so cool that when they passed by, all you could say was, "Frosty!" They tended to be more educated and somewhat more affluent than the patrons of other clubs.

Then there was the Beverly Gardens. It wasn't earthy like the Owl's Club. It wasn't sophisticated (frosty) like the Diplomat. The best way to describe the Beverly Gardens was "greasy"—and I mean that with the greatest respect and affection. The thing I remember most about the Beverly Gardens was that it was usually open later than the other two clubs and it sold the best fried chicken. Those who still had the party spirit after the Owl's Club and the Diplomat closed would find their way out to Sweet Home.

The one thing all these clubs had in common was their patrons' appreciation for good soul music and a funky good time. In fact, it was in the uniqueness of their differences that we found their common threads. As much as those differences were about class and style, or the influence of culture, in the end a club was always about the music. And that's where we, the Jades, came in. We had to be able to play to all those crowds, sometimes all in the same night! Some mornings we would get home just before the sun rose, and when our heads hit our pillows, they would be vibrating from all the sounds from the night before. That's the only time I think we prayed that those moments would hurry on by.

## CHAPTER 12

# A Change Was Going to Come

*Somebody pinch me,* I'd say to myself. *Can it get any better than this? No way!* We were living in the moment and we knew it. We were too young to know, or even to care, that when something seems too good to be true, it usually is.

It was getting late in the fall. John had joined Patrick on tour with Up with People, and even though Leonard had taken his place, there seemed to be something in the wind, something lurking in the shadows. It wasn't a physical something; it was more like an unspoken or unacknowledged something. And while for the most part we were able to ignore it, it was always there. A change was coming, and there was nothing anybody could do to stop it.

On Thanksgiving Day, our school marching band had to play at our annual football classic. It was so cold that day I believe polar bears would have stayed at home. It was so cold that our band director, Mr. Sterling Ingram, told us that we shouldn't try to play our instruments on the field; we should just march to the beat of the drum. For Mr. Ingram to do that, it had to be cold.

The whole time we were performing, our minds were on the gig that we were going to play that night in Morrilton, Arkansas. If it was this cold in the daytime, what on earth would it be like when the sun went down? Unfortunately, we found out. It was so cold that if you sneezed, you would have sneezed snowflakes. And when we arrived at the gymnasium where we were going to perform, we were terrified. It looked like most of the windows in the place had been knocked out. How in the world were we supposed to play in those conditions? We were surprised to find that the building actually had electricity and gas. There were two space heaters in the whole building, and thank goodness they were placed on the floor on either side of the stage.

When it comes to having a good time, teenagers are like postmen: "Neither rain, nor sleet, nor snow can stop them from their appointed rounds." By the time we got cranked up good, the place was hotter than a firecracker on the Fourth of July. The Incredible Jades were incredible again.

On the way back, as tired as we were, we were still reveling in how well we had been received—and then, out of nowhere, there "it" was again. Yacky made a comment about how he was going to miss this because he was going into the service after graduation, and to my surprise, Scooter said he was thinking about enlisting too.

Sure, we had felt it—we knew it was out there—but we'd hoped that if we never spoke about it, maybe it would go away. But now, after riding high on the mountaintop, we came crashing down to the valley. What had never been said was now all over us like a blanket, trying to smother us. Something was happening to our moment. A change was going to come.

# CHAPTER 13

# The End of Innocence

While we were wrestling with change that we did not want to see, change was happening all around us. The music of the late sixties was a celebration of change throughout our country. The music industry had long been dominated and controlled by the white establishment, but when the likes of Motown and Stax Records came on the scene, black entertainers were no longer left without alternatives.

We as a people were shouting with James Brown, "Say it loud—I'm black and I'm proud!" This new mindset was everywhere. Afros were being worn not as fashion statements, but as symbols of our newly liberated spirits. I wanted to wear an afro too, but while I was letting it grow, my dad came up to me and volunteered to cut it for me, which I correctly interpreted to mean "Get a haircut or I will cut it for you." I still had memories of his last attempt to cut my hair some years before. Oh well—I still had the music.

It wasn't that we were isolated from the events of our time, because we were not. But their impact was somewhat tempered by the fact that we attended an all-black high school, Horace Mann High, and all our friends lived in black neighborhoods. Our contact with the white community was limited. Of course, when we went downtown, there were signs intended to keep us in our place: For Whites Only signs were everywhere, and For Colored Only signs were strategically placed over water fountains, bathroom doors, and lunch counters too. But as segregated as things were, when it came to good music, the whites wanted to hear us as much as, if not more than, our own people did.

We got our first white gig at a place called the Silver Hook. We had never played to an all-white audience before, but we soon learned that they got just as juiced as black folks, and when they did, they were just as rowdy. There was one difference, though: when they got to feeling no pain, they would come up to us and stick money in our horns. And I didn't have any problem with that at all.

Because we were able to improvise (that's what professionals called making music up on the spot), we were able to fool white folks into thinking we knew how to play their brand of music. We eventually added a few country-and-western tunes to our playlist for just those kinds of occasions.

Now we were truly playing everywhere. Some nights we would leave a club at one in the morning and go to another and play until four or five. I remember how much I hated to see the sunrise; it always spelled trouble.

One night we were coming back from Hot Springs, Arkansas, where we had performed at the ritzy Hot Springs Yacht Club. Those folks had more money than Carter had liver pills—and they didn't mind sharing it. We made as much again in tips as we did for the whole gig. We were some truly happy people that night.

I guess this is a good time to point out that we were driving back to Little Rock in our Al Capone-style black limousine, the Jade Mobile, with the long running boards. I point this out because at four in the morning, a long black limousine loaded down with a bunch of black males in it would look suspicious to anybody out that late to see it.

The state police were not only out—they were everywhere. At first there was just one car in front of us; then another one came up behind us. We didn't think much of it at first, except that some of the guys rolled down their windows and flipped them the bird. That was not a very good idea. The troopers behind us got so close that we could actually see their faces, even that late at night. Another trooper came alongside us and told us to pull over. What had started out as a stupid little prank had quickly escalated into major trouble, or so we thought.

We were scared, and that was just what they wanted us to be. One officer asked Mr. Thomas where we were going so early in the morning, and he said that we had just come back from performing at the Yacht Club and were on our way home. The officer then asked him to open up the U-Haul so they could inspect it. When Mr. Thomas asked why, the answer the officer gave us was not one any of us was prepared for. He said that Dr. Martin Luther King had been assassinated, and they wanted to make sure that we were in fact musicians and not some gang coming into town to stir up trouble.

The magnitude of that news was beyond our comprehension. I'm not sure that it really sank in. We were dizzy with disbelief. Not another word was spoken among us all the way home. The state police escorted each of us to our doorsteps and said good night.

There would be no good nights for decades to come. We had not been shielded from our times, but this event took whatever innocence we had and shattered it.

# Chapter 14

# The Last Dance

It was late spring now, and prom season was just around the corner. We had a very full calendar, and so we had to make sure that none of the proms that we were engaged to play conflicted with our own. I think we were excited that we were actually going to get a break; being rock stars was hard work. Okay, we weren't really rock stars, but we really did need the break.

When prom night finally arrived, we brought our girls and our axes too. Why? I don't know; I guess some habits are hard to break. The band that had been hired to play for us was—how I can say it?—not *us*. They were okay, but that was it. Just okay. Their sound was too fragmented. Their solos were too low. Their singers didn't have the voices. They didn't have uniforms. They didn't have moves. They just weren't us. I think our egos told us that we were better, and no one could convince us otherwise.

When the band took its first intermission, we went and got our instruments. We were determined to show those guys how a real band was supposed to sound. It wasn't long, though, before our dates reminded us that they were the ones who needed entertaining, not the rest of the crowd. When I think back on that time, I realize that we were a band gone wild and didn't know it.

We made it through the rest of the prom without any more antics, but it was hard.

It was now approaching graduation day. Like all the other seniors, we were excited about finishing up high school and facing the rest of the world. The only problem for us was that graduation meant coming to grips with the reality that some of us would be moving on to new challenges that did not include the Jades.

Even though we were able to play together for most of that summer, time was winding down. Growing up was a bummer. Why did things have to change? Yacky and Scooter did go off to join the service. I went off to college. David remained in town, but he married his high school sweetheart, Wanda, and grew up real fast. He was able to keep part of the group together, because Granvel, Joe, and Cheryl were just rising seniors. The guys who replaced us were very good, and I was proud of what David had done to keep the band going and make good music. They still had a sound—a great sound that was worthy of being the Incredible Jades—but as wonderful as that sound was, it was not *our* sound. We had played our last dance.

The moment that had shone so bright, the moment that had taken us to places we had never dreamed of, the moment that we would have liked to savor forever— that moment had ended at last.

# CHAPTER 15

# Déjà Vu

Remember how I told you I thought we were *gooood*? Well, I really did think that, and when I went off to Jarvis Christian College in Hawkins, Texas, I carried a cassette of one of our live performances to keep those moments close to me.

One day I was listening to it while studying, and one of my roommates asked me where I got the compilation recording. I told him that it was a recording of the group that I used to be part of. My roommate refused to believe that I could have played in a band that sounded so original. All I could do was say it really was my group.

When word got out that I was claiming to have played in a really hot band, the rest of my roommates said, "Prove it."

As fortune would have it, I was president of my freshman class, and as such, one of my responsibilities was to find ways to raise funds for our class activities. What better way to raise money than to put on a concert and dance? We had been washing cars to help raise money, so I knew we had enough set aside to pay to get the group there, and I knew that by splitting the proceeds from the door, we could take care of everything else.

When you have more than five hundred students on campus in a town that has only one stop sign and one flashing red light, when there are more people living on campus than in the town, and it's a campus with nothing else to do, what you really have is a captive audience. So I calculated that at five dollars a head, even if only half the campus showed up, we would raise enough to take care of the group. I knew this because whenever there was any social function on campus, almost everyone showed up. And if there was a live band, I knew the place would be packed. My fundraising/publicity committee did a good job of getting the word out, and sure enough, the night of the dance, the student union was packed to capacity.

In show business, presentation is everything. When the guys arrived on campus, they pulled up in front of the student union in the Jade Mobile and trailer along with another Cadillac and trailer. The group had not only expanded but also acquired much more equipment designed to add to the dramatics of the show. For the first time, there were multicolored floodlights and strobe lights, more and larger speakers and accompanying amplifiers, and several more microphones. I have to say that I, too, was impressed by what David had done with the group. When they showed up they had two drummers, Scooter and his soon-to-be replacement, and two saxophonists—my replacement on tenor and an alto. Those two guys were really cooking with gas. There was a replacement for Yacky on bass, and of course the rest of the guys were there too—David, Joe, Cheryl, and Leonard.

When we took the stage, it was like *Showtime at the Apollo*—we blew their minds. We put on a show the likes of which they had never seen. Cheryl was dazzling, our uniforms were sparkling, and the saxes were blowing and going. In the past when I would play a solo, I had David and Granvel to provide backup, but now, with the addition of the two saxes, the sound was hammering! My roommates just fell over themselves. To say the least, I made believers out of them. The girls were screaming and hollering, and the joint was jamming.

And here we go again: when anyone tells you that something is too good to be true, trust me—it usually is. The night was going great. One of my committee members came to me and told me that we had raised more than enough money to pay the band, and just as that message was being delivered to me—déjà vu—the campus chief of security came in, pulled out a starter pistol, pointed it at the ceiling, and fired. He declared the dance an unlawful assembly and demanded that everyone vacate the premises. Apparently there had been some serious altercation outside that prompted him to take that action. Of course, this meant that we had to refund everyone (with the exception of the freshmen in attendance) their money. I couldn't believe it—wasn't this how we'd started? Who would have thought that such a thing could happen again. *Pinch me!* I thought. *Wake me up! Tell me it ain't so!* I couldn't be the one to do this to the group. But I was, and I did.

You should have seen the looks on their faces. They had come all those miles, and the crowd had seen the dazzling lights and heard a sound system that shook the building's very foundation. The Jades had mesmerized people with a performance they would talk about for weeks to come, and there was no pay.

For me it was a living nightmare, my worst fears come true. All we could do was pay for the guys' gas to get them back to Arkansas and feed them a little something before they left. I think I was more devastated than they were. In fact, David and the guys, while obviously disappointed, were more than understanding and actually started laughing. Oh, they let me know that when they got back to Little Rock they would talk about me for days. But they let me off the hook.

Because of their love for me, the group turned what otherwise would have been a major catastrophe into a memory that we would always look back on with fondness and laughter.

I was, to say the least, the big man on campus after that weekend performance, despite how it had ended. It was nice to get the attention, even though it was fleeting. What was really great was being able to extend the moment for one last time.

Some moments come and go, but the best ones last a lifetime. This was such a moment.

The Jades perform on various programs for the school and community. The Jades consist of: David Bynum, trumpet; William Thrasher, saxaphone; Granvel Hadley, trumpet; George Mitchell, drums; Donald Jenkins, bass guitar; John Reeves, organ; Joe Thomas, electric guitar.

William Trasher and David Bynum, along with
the rest of the group, participated in the Victory
Ball social after the homecoming game.

William Trasher, John Reeves, Donald
Jenkins, and David Bynum played with
the group in the all boy's assembly.

The Jades set the students' souls on fire.

# The Jade Mobile

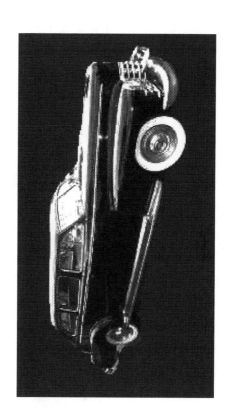

Printed in the United States
By Bookmasters